CW00683712

P R ~

A WONDERFU

"The title of this book may sound like a bold statement in our tumultuous and changing world! In ten chapters Sue explains why these words hold a universal truth and conveys them in a way that we can understand very clearly.

Each chapter is captivating, informative, positive and filled with Sue's knowledge and sheer love for life. Most importantly it contains the nuts and bolts of our ascension process, which is gaining vast momentum around the world as millions wake up and begin to look for answers. The light level is rising so quickly that many people are finding themselves in need of guidance so that they may step up themselves.

The role of modern spirituality may seem quite confusing with so much information to choose from. When you take away the unnecessary distractions you are left with a simple course of action…raise your vibration and be the good that you wish to see in the world. Sue explains this so beautifully. Sue Stone is an incredible lady who has achieved the very best of her life pathway and is loving every second of it! This book is empowering and inspirational as she is."

TIM WHILD

Author, International Speaker and Spiritual Leader
www.timwhild.com

"For anyone caught up in a fear based narrative, stop "doom scrolling" and step into your power! There is no one better to remind us how to do this than Sue Stone; she is literally a ray of sunshine and positivity.

Sue makes the "woo woo" accessible and the impossible feel not only possible, but right within our grasp. Top up your battery levels with this book that may be short, but packs a punch. Sue shares effective tips and techniques to help keep us grounded and focused, yet our vibration high. I use her mantra "I love life and life loves me" many times a day, it sure beats being miserable and stressing out!"

JANEY LEE GRACE

Author and Presenter
Founder of www.thesoberclub.com

A WONDERFUL WORLD FOR ALL!

A Practical Guide

BY SUE STONE

First published in January 2023

© Sue Stone 2023

A catalogue record for this book is available from the British Library.

ISBN: 978-1-915787-31-6

Printed in Great Britain by
Biddles Books Limited, King's Lynn, Norfolk

HUGE GRATITUDE TO MY AMAZING CONTRIBUTORS;

Diana Cooper, World Spiritual Teacher and Author
www.dianacooper.com

Pam Gregory, Master Astrologer and Author
www.pamgregory.com

Dr. Sam White, Functional Medical Doctor
www.drsamwhite.com

About the Author

Human Potential and Transformational Leader of the Sue Stone Foundation, Sue Stone is recognised as the UK's happiest and most positive person..... a far cry from many years ago when she had forgotten what it felt like to be happy.

From £10 left in her purse, depressed, desperate and full of fear to becoming totally at peace, happy, financially free and a TV Secret Millionaire, Sue has gone through an incredible life transformation.

Author and inspirational speaker, Sue dedicates her life to helping others. She is regularly in the media, a TV presenter and thrives on helping people from all walks of life across the world to create a life they love with personal empowerment, inspirational business mentoring and motivational speaking.

In 2011 Sue set up the Sue Stone Foundation to truly make a difference across the world. She has a growing global team of Accredited Coaches within the SSF, who give one to one and group workshop sessions and talks. These encompass an expansive range of personal obstacles and challenges that are faced by individuals from all walks of life.

For contact details, other products available or to book Sue please visit www.suestone.com.

To join Sue's team in the Sue Stone Foundation or to find an accredited coach to help you please visit www.suestonefoundation.com.

CONTENTS

INTRODUCTION

My hope and intention behind this book is to encourage and empower as many as possible to join together and co-create a better world for everyone.

Many people believe, me included, that this is an incredible time to be alive!

We are here to witness the breaking down of the old ways and systems, as we as a whole, go through the ascension process to create a far better, fairer, equal and kinder world for everyone.

Is this really possible? What does this all mean? How can we get there?

Part of our journey to a more wonderful world is the discovery of new capacities, new sources of information and solutions, not only to the questions that we have today, but to the questions that will crop up as we journey into the future.

So I would like to welcome especially that part of you that just doesn't know how it is possible to create a wonderful world for all, and the part of you that is willing not to know for now, because that not knowing creates a vacuum, an empty space into which genuinely new knowledge and wisdom can flow.

So welcome to all of that and welcome to this book wherein I share what I have discovered so far!

1.
IT'S UP TO US!

When I hit my emotional and financial rock bottom in 1999, what I now refer to as my "wake up" call, I remember saying to myself "Sue Stone, if you don't do something to help yourself and turn your life around, no one is going to do it for you!" I decided to take 100% responsibility and started researching ways to change my life for the better.... the rest is history.

I have been openly sharing over 2 decades the exciting knowledge I discovered, how I applied it in my life (which enabled my own life transformation) in my passion to help others achieve happiness, inner peace and their dreams too.

Along the way though I also discovered some disturbing truths and saw through many of the illusions of how the world works and the many fear-based systems borne out of control and greed. I am not going to give too much attention and energy to the "negatives", but I do want to touch on just a few here as educating myself in these areas I have found to be very empowering. In the beginning though I found much of it quite shocking and almost incredulous.

Let us take the banking system, for example, most people do not know this, but when you borrow money the banks literally create money out of thin air; if you default, they suffer no real loss, yet pursue you relentlessly for the so called debt, creating huge fear, loss and mental health issues. Having faced repossession of my own home years back and having represented myself in court as a Litigant in Person, I know how terrifying that is, hence my passion for raising awareness and helping others in this area.

Did you know that your government is a corporation? Its agencies are corporations, law enforcement agencies, including police forces in Britain, are corporations and the courts are corporations...... all private *for-profit* corporations!

I'm not going to elaborate further in this book but it is certainly food for thought when you start to understand what all this actually means.

There is so much more at a global level too, but if you are not mindful it is very easy to slip into depression, despair and hopelessness that come when you really start to understand the workings of power, or should I say old power, in this world.

Going back to that time in my life when I was desperate and consumed with fear, I have to be honest, I had no care for what was going on in the outside world, I was too consumed with my own personal mini world of chaos and drama.

If *your* world is not flowing as you would like it to right now, I encourage you to embrace the following that I discovered and researched over many years and applied into my life.

I began to understand that there is a much bigger picture to life than the everyday challenges that we all face. I learnt about the power of our thoughts and feelings and about our conscious and subconscious minds and the universal laws that exist. I also learnt about the incredible power that is within every single one of us, and I have realised as time has gone by that so few people have any understanding of this power and have yet to develop and use it to its full potential.

Understanding and learning to consciously implement the power of our thoughts and emotions is a vital and necessary component to accomplishing and achieving a life of inner peace and joy.

The more I read and understood, I realised that it was me that had to make a major shift in my thinking and that the reason I was in my awful situation was that I had "created" (unconsciously) the situation in the first place! It was hard to take onboard at first but a lack of money or the fear of something going wrong was often in the back of my mind.

Often people have no conscious awareness (like me at the time) of how their life has got so bad! The "real truth" is that those circumstances are being created because that is what they are thinking or fearing at some level! The fact that they regularly think about what's negative or lacking is enough to allow the subconscious mind to begin the process of what it is designed to do; it absorbs the thought as truth, stores it and begins the process that will actually cause it to happen in the physical world.

When your thoughts are reinforced with emotions and words, it actually speeds up the process of materialisation.

Many times, although they may consciously desire one outcome their predominant focus is placed on what they DON'T have or what they fear and as a result experience more of what they DON'T want.

What is crucial to understand is this. If you choose to have an abundant, happy and harmonious life, your predominant thoughts and emotions and the words you speak need to be focused on and in harmony with what it is you desire and NOT what is lacking.

We can dramatically improve the quality of our lives by taking control of our minds and manufacturing beliefs and expectations consistent with what we want to happen in the future.

Remember, you are what you think you are and you become what you say.

When you establish the belief that something will happen, the vibrational frequency of the power of thought, more specifically the emotion that these thoughts create and ignite, will draw to you more experiences aligned with that vibrational frequency.

The key to remember here is that two things in vibrational resonance with each other are drawn together. That is proven by science and your feelings reveal to you the vibration you are on.

So if we think thoughts of what we don't want or what we are fearing, it is bound to make us *feel* negative and fearful and, quite effortlessly and often unconsciously, we draw more things to us to make us feel that way again.

A hugely powerful and simple phrase to remember is "the way I *feel* in *every* moment is what I am creating for my future".

It is OK to have a negative thought but remember not to feed it, it's like throwing fuel on the fire, as a negative thought only has power if you react to it and give it emotion.

The thing about this is that everybody is always right! The negative thinkers say "I knew it would go wrong" or "I knew it wouldn't work" and the positive thinkers say "I knew I'd find a way" or "I knew the solution would present itself".

It is important to shift with lots of tiny steps into becoming "solution conscious" as opposed to "problem conscious", to being in a state of gratitude and love for the good in your life *right now*, however small it may appear, rather than being in a state of fear and lack.

It really does need to be a *moment by moment* awareness, especially in the beginning. Become the "observer" of yourself and ask yourself regularly throughout the day "What am I thinking? What am I feeling? What am I saying?".

Remember, every thought you think, every emotion you have and every word you speak affects you at the energetic (quantum) level.

It's all about your state of "BEing" in the NOW, in this moment.

In *every* moment you are radiating energy (in fact you ARE energy) out into the universe and physics says your outgoing signal is *always* matched by the incoming one.

Remember every one of us today in this moment is the "product" of our previous programming, conditioning, experiences, culture etc and this is what makes up our consciousness, our energy field, our vibration.

Very simply put our consciousness is made up of;-

Our thoughts
our intentions
our feelings
our beliefs about ourselves and
our beliefs about life

These beliefs can be very positive ones or very negative ones, or something in between and very often borne out of what can appear to be very real "truths" at times. These are supported by your life experiences and in particular your programming as a child, which is a time when you were particularly open and would easily absorb the beliefs and attitudes of your parents, role models and teachers.

The truth is that you are creating your reality of a world that surrounds you, a bubble of experience which accompanies you wherever you go.

The existence of these little individual worlds we all have, accounts for people having such different experiences even when they are in the same location. Some people perceive life as joyful, safe and loving, and others see it as dangerous and full of anger and hatred. If these are the qualities which dominate their consciousness, then this is what will permeate their bubble of reality and colour their experience.

Your outer world is a reflection of your inner world and in modern Western cultures, people generally do not see this connection between the two, they tend to project judgement and blame outwards onto other people. They criticise and blame their partner, their children, their boss, their rival, their enemy, indeed anyone except themselves for the difficulties and disasters that befall them.

We have been conditioned to believe that we are separate from the world. If more people only knew that they have the power within them to shift their consciousness and that they are not weak, helpless and powerless victims of circumstances.

I can understand that there are many who do blame the governments of our world for their unprecedented attempts at control in 2020 and 2021; however the positive side is it has proven to be a catalyst for earth's ascension (explained in Chapter 3), leading to a mass awakening whereby many more souls are questioning everything that plays out on the world stage.

It is an exciting time in our history as so many are recognising that we are all a connected family on this planet....... it has also been proven mathematically that *every* cell in our universe is connected to *every* single other one.....and that it is very much time to come together in co-operation and collaboration and co-create a wonderful world that makes all our hearts sing!

We are not powerLESS victims in our universe, we are hugely powerFULL co-creators!

For those that may have a religious background, you will discover if you choose to delve deeply enough that what has been discovered by modern day science is precisely what the great spiritual teachers of the world have shared and attempted to get their followers to understand for thousands upon thousands of years.

The conclusions that have been arrived at thus far through the study of Quantum Physics align perfectly with what all the major religions of the world have always taught in some form.

Science and Theology are in fact closing in on each other. Science is saying that everything is energy and everything is vibrating. Everything has its own vibrational frequency and resonance. Science says energy is: "on the surface of universal consciousness which is omnipresent." Theology says, "God is everywhere –omnipresence".

The continuing studies can blow your mind away, every time scientists go looking for more, they find it! If you are interested in going deeper and further, I urge you to do your own research.

Please also note that there are still many different interpretations of quantum theory; what is for certain is that we will learn much more in the coming decades about the mechanics of how we create our own reality.

The fact that we are able to do it, however, is proven beyond doubt.

2.

HEAL OURSELVES WE HEAL THE WORLD

"When we heal ourselves, we heal the world; for as the body is only as healthy as its individual cells, the world is only as healthy as its individual souls."

Mark Nepo

As I came through the transition of healing from my past and understanding all that I now share, my passion and care for others in the world and for the greater good emerged.

You can make a real difference in the world in ways you may not be aware of. You are an integral part of the whole of existence.

There is wisdom, healing and an integration that happens through dedicating an adequate amount of time to our own healing, transformation and empowerment; this, I believe, is an important part of a balanced path in creating a better world.

Many people, often very sensitive and empathic ones, still have a hard time grasping this because they see others suffering in the world and have a great desire to help them before themselves.

The analogy of the oxygen mask comes to mind. When you travel on an aeroplane, if there is an incident of low cabin pressure, the flight attendant will instruct you to put your own oxygen mask on yourself before you try and help others put their mask on. The reason for this is that if you try and help someone else get their mask on before you put yours on, there is a possibility that you could both pass out from lack of oxygen. If, however, you first put your mask on yourself, you are then able to focus on helping others who may need your help.

Similarly, we all have "oxygen masks" in our own life. Our oxygen masks are our energy, time and resources. If we fill our own tank first, we then have the ability to use our reserves to help other people.

If you wish to see more empathic leaders, so that our world becomes more equal and less divisive with more kindness and compassion in the world, it makes so much sense to take care, heal and empower yourself.

You as one person is one cell of this entire organism. This organism being life, life on Earth, we are all connected and just like in your body, all your cells are connected. They are all part of your body.

When you look at yourself you see an individual person. But if you understand the nature of who you are, you realise that you are actually a community of about 50 trillion living cells. Each cell is a living individual, a sentient being that has its own life and functions but interacts with other cells in the nature of a community.

If I could reduce you to the size of a cell and drop you inside your own body, you would see a very busy metropolis of trillions of individuals living within one skin. This becomes relevant when we understand that health is when there is harmony in the community and dis-ease is when there is a disharmony that tends to fracture the community relationships.

If one cell is sick and it spreads to the other cells, that sickness spreads, but if one cell is super healthy and lifts up the other cells around it, wellness spreads. Be a spreader of wellness!

If you don't heal your past trauma, you can end up looking at life and the world through a trauma lens. You can also end up interpreting things through the eyes of a victim as if things are happening to you, instead of things happening for you.

Heal and empower yourself and get into a position of *knowing* that we are creators of our world, as opposed to reacting to the world outside.

We all go through positive and negative experiences during our lives and unfortunately, many people hang on to or constantly recall those negative experiences, some of which go back years, perhaps even all the way back to childhood.

Other unpleasant or negative situations may have happened yesterday or six months ago. Something someone did may have angered you, caused you to build up resentment, seek revenge etc. When you hold on to these negative experiences you actually block your ability to move forward and heal. Anger and resentment drains your energy and keeps you imprisoned in your past.

There is a true physical relationship between your emotions and your nervous system, endocrine system and immune system.

What you think and feel turns into the chemistry, biology and the immunity of your body. So much of what goes on in your body is under the control of peptides and receptors.

When you feel happy and joyful, your brain produces happy, joyful peptides and when you are angry or anxious your brain produces angry/anxious peptides.

Peptides travel to your cells and enter them through doorway-like receptors and influence many of the cells actions. For example, you may go white as a sheet when you are scared or bright red when you are embarrassed or angry.

Every hour of every day millions of cell divisions occur in your body to replace the old cells that die. If you feel negative and anxious for an hour, they have produced millions of new cells that are more sensitive to negative anxious peptides....creating a body that is more apt to anxiety rather than joy.

Our body is remaking itself all the time so it makes sense to create the best possible emotional health that you can. Love and gratitude are hugely powerful and simply smiling, laughing and hugging keep your body in a state of emotional equilibrium.

Forgiveness is an incredibly powerful, self-liberating and healing principle, which, when properly implemented, allows a sense of peace and overall wellbeing to flow and permeate your innermost being. Many people do not appreciate that when someone makes the choice to hold resentment or "un-forgiveness" against another, they are not hurting the person that they are holding the resentment against, but instead only hurting themselves.

Normally we think of forgiveness as us forgiving others who we perceive have "wronged" us in some way. However, it is equally as important to develop the ability to forgive yourself for past mistakes that you have made and perceive and hold as guilt.

It is important to consider what forgiveness does NOT mean. Forgiveness does not mean you allow people to treat you badly. Forgiveness does not mean you are condoning or excusing the person's behaviour and does not mean that you have to trust that person again. Remember, forgiveness is more for you than the other person.

By choosing to forgive and let go of your hurt and anger you give yourself the freedom to fully heal and experience joy in life.

In my book "The Power Within You Now!" I share a number of Self Transformational Tools and at the end of this chapter I have included two incredibly powerful but simple-to-use techniques that I love.

Everything you do, think and feel affects the people in your lives and their reactions in turn affect others. The choices you make have far-reaching consequences.

Your energy is contagious! It will either affect people in a positive way or it will infect people in a negative way.

Each of us carries within us the capacity to change the world in small ways for better or worse. Once we get our "inner world" joyful and peaceful our "outer world" reflects that back to us.

To be quite honest though, as I mentioned previously, when I was living in a state of fear and "drama" all those years ago, I truly did not care what was going on in the world; I was totally focused on my own survival. I urge people to not wait until they are as desperate as I was before they start to work on themselves and understand just how powerful we ALL are.

The "collective consciousness" permeates all of us, affecting our attitudes, feelings and behaviours. We are all a part of the whole, just like cells within the body, as I mentioned above. They function separately, but also work together as the basis of life itself.

Just as the collective consciousness can impact you; you too can influence the collective consciousness for the better.

You are a powerful spiritual being, with far-reaching influence. The vibrations you put out at any given moment, affect the collective consciousness of all beings, in much the same way a tiny pebble causes large ripples upon the water.

As you transmit the higher vibrational energies of gratitude, love and peace to the universe, those energies permeate the collective whole, transforming and healing the world on a cosmic level. Not only that, the energy you send out into the universe is also returned to you.

You can not only help heal the world, but you can also become a magnet for healing, peace and joy in your own life and the people around you. You can do this regularly in just a few minutes per day.

Focus (or meditate) on sending peace, healing and love to those in need; you too will become a healthier, more joyful person. In just moments a day, you can make a difference in your own life and the lives of others. Just like that pebble, your intention can cast ripples into the consciousness of humanity.

*****

Powerful Transformational Tools

One of the simplest and most powerful healing tools that I love to share is Ho'oponopono. It is a self transformational technique that can work miracles.

Ho'oponopono (meaning to "make right") is an ancestral Hawaiian practice that was used as a form of family therapy. This old Hawaiian practice was simplified and adapted by Mornah Simeona and has been popularized by people, such as the late Dr. Hew Len and Joe Vitale who featured in The Secret. The practice is so simple and so powerful that it is difficult to believe the results one can achieve.

Ho'oponopono can be learned in 5 minutes, implemented immediately and practiced anywhere, anytime. It's a simple form of mantra, affirmation or prayer (call it as you like) that doesn't require adopting a new belief system, it's not bound to any religion and encompasses love, responsibility, respect, forgiveness, faith and gratitude.

We are the sum total of all our experiences and when we experience stress or fear in our lives, if we were to look carefully, we would find that the cause is actually a memory. It is the emotions which are tied to these memories that affect us now.

What this process does, quite simply, is clean the data, which is stored subconsciously. Mornah Simeona describes the main purpose of it is to discover the Divinity within oneself. She believes it is a profound gift which allows one to develop a working relationship with the Divinity within and as we do it our errors in thought, word, deed or action are cleansed.

It has proven so effective that she taught it at the United Nations, the World Health Organisation and institutions of healing throughout the world.

A big part of Ho'oponopono is about taking personal responsibility and the understanding that "peace begins with me". The world is a reflection of what is happening inside us. If you are experiencing upset or imbalance, the place to look is inside yourself, not outside at the object you perceive as causing your problem. All that takes place in your life is created by your memories be it at a conscious, subconscious, cellular or soul level.

Every stress and imbalance can be corrected just by working on yourself. Ho'oponopono permits you to clear away your memories. Memories are not intrinsically bad or good; we make that judgement about them. It may be that the memory of an event seemed good for years (for example, a marriage) but we now remember it as bad (it ended in divorce).

Some memories appear to be false and others seem accurate. However, they are all only memories that need to be cleansed of the negative emotion so you can be free of them. Ho'oponopono makes this possible.

The Mantra and how this cleansing is performed.

"I love you, I'm sorry, please forgive me, thank you"

Some people choose to start with "I'm sorry" but I agree with Joe Vitale that when you start with "I love you", you are immediately connecting to your higher self and I find this to be more powerful.

You begin with "I love you", it immediately creates that connection to your higher self, only love can heal and when you say this you are speaking to both your memories and yourself.

Then you say "I'm sorry" because you were unaware that you carried that memory inside of yourself or sorry for your part to play in this (at some level).

Then you say "Please forgive me" to the divinity you carry within yourself and ask the divinity for assistance in self-forgiveness that you allowed these memories to "lead you astray".

Next you say "Thank you" to your memories for appearing to you and thus giving you the opportunity to free yourself of them. You also thank the divine and your inner divinity for helping you in this liberation.

This process is to forgive yourself, thank yourself and send yourself love. By doing this you erase the impact of the memory. As the suffering vanishes from within you, it also disappears from the other person or the situation. When you speak these words you are addressing yourself, specifically the young child within you who is in pain.

You have nothing to do or understand other than just to say these words.

Anytime you have a trigger of a negative emotion, gently repeat the mantra for as long as you feel is necessary.

This is particularly what I love about the simplicity of Ho'oponopono. It is no longer necessary to hunt for the source of a disruptive memory, the painful event surrounding its origin.

The process can seem difficult to the mind, only because the mind wants to control and understand everything. But your mind is useful in this process and plays an important role. The mind has its own free will and it can make the decision to let go of all control and power and place its trust in the inner divinity to clean out and therefore free you of your memories. The intellect mind gives way to the intuition of the heart.

Tapping the Thymus Gland

Here's another quick self-transformational healing tool for your total well-being mind, body and soul; tapping the Thymus Gland. I recommend doing this daily as part of your getting up routine.

The Thymus Gland was named from the Greek word "thymus" which literally translates into "life energy".

The Thymus is located in the middle of our chests, just above our breasts, you know when you've found the spot, it can feel slightly sensitive.

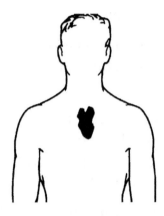

It is responsible for manufacturing and releasing T-cells which are an important component of our immune system. T-cells are involved in our overall wellness, helping our bodies to resist diseases like cancer.

The thymus is a major part of our immune system. In addition, the thymus also creates a connection between mind and body and is sensitive to emotion, stress and negativity.

When we experience high levels of stress, negativity and an imbalance of emotions we are more prone to illness. One thing we can do to increase health and wellbeing in our bodies, even in times of great stress, is to stimulate the thymus gland.

Tapping the thymus boosts energy, relieves stress and increases strength and vitality and is a part of many ancient healing traditions.

For a speedy burst of energy, tap your thymus with your fingertips for 20 seconds, while slowly and deeply breathing in and out.

Don't tap too hard. You only need gentle tapping to stimulate the thymus gland.

Some experts suggest that in order to have the most energising effect tap in the waltz beat, a one-two-three count, with the emphasis on the first count, repeating the affirmation «My life energy is high, I am full of love».

In addition to strengthening the immune response in your body, this technique can also be helpful in pain reduction and can be used as and when required.

As you tap you can say some of your own positive affirmations, for example, "I am healthy, mentally emotionally and physically" but I particularly wanted to share it with you in this chapter as it is a powerful way to release any fears and blocks that you may not be consciously aware of.

I was shown this by a very gifted spiritual teacher and friend, Donna Maxine (www.donnamaxine.com) and the mantra she taught me to use while tapping, which I did every morning as part of my daily routine, is as follows;-

"I now willingly and lovingly release any fears and blocks that I may have at a conscious and subconscious level, through all time and space that may be holding me back at this time, and I now willingly and lovingly step into my greatest, happiest, blissful and most abundant and healthy self" (or whatever positive words you may choose to use there that resonate with you).

Of course, as you say it, you can add fears and blocks around money, or fears and blocks around relationships or your health or whatever you feel is relevant to you in the moment.

You can also tap on the thymus gland to work on releasing any childhood, past life, collective or inherited cell memories that you may or may not be aware of as follows;-

NB only use the words that you feel are relevant to you.

"I now willingly and lovingly release any past life and inherited ancestral memories, childhood traumas or negative pain memories that are holding me back, from every cell in my body and layer of my aura and transmute them in the violet flame".

Take a deep breath and exhale.

When our life energy is vibrant and strong, our awareness and our connection to source are enhanced and we are more empowered to embrace the Ascension process too.

3.
WHAT IS THE ASCENSION PROCESS?

Many people are confused about what Ascension means when it is referred to in the spiritual sense. Ascension can mean different things to many people. The literal definition of the word ascension means: the act of ascending or ascent; to be risen up or to climb.

The concept of Ascension itself can be explained in several different contexts depending on the spiritual tradition or philosophy or metaphysical system.

Ascension, in a simple and spiritual sense is very similar to the Eastern concept of Enlightenment found in Buddhism. To become enlightened can simply mean to have "full comprehension of a situation". Enlightenment is a spiritual revelation or deep insight into the meaning and purpose of all things. It is a profound spiritual understanding or a fundamentally changed consciousness, whereby everything is perceived as an interconnected unity.

Ascension in its basic spiritual or mystical sense can be thought of as the highest state of man (humanity). It is the expansion of awareness. It involves the realisation of being One with the Creator and all of creation.

An individual is "ascending" in the sense that something of a lower vibration is ascending; it is being "raised up" or becoming higher in vibration. This is why many spiritual traditions aim to achieve the dissolution of the human ego (lower self) in order to realise the true nature of their being or Higher Self.

Ascension is about "bringing heaven" to earth by raising the lower vibrational aspect of your non-physical being to a higher vibrational state of being or realisation.

Ascension can also be understood in a more metaphysical way by considering the concept of dimensions or planes of existence or planes of consciousness. This would mean that Ascension is about shifting from one dimension, frequency and plane of existence or consciousness to another plane, dimension or state of consciousness that is of a higher frequency.

At this present time, every life form on this planet is undergoing a rapid evolutionary process. The Ascension process and the signs and symptoms associated with it are occurring on a personal and planetary level as a whole.

On an individual level ascension involves changing one's consciousness from one reality, based on one set of beliefs, to another. On a group or planetary level, ascension is the collective expansion of a state of consciousness (set of beliefs) to the point where that consciousness creates and shifts into a new reality—a new state of being, paradigm or dimension.

When we choose to expand our awareness (or as it happens naturally), our overall vibration becomes lighter/higher. We are then able to tune into higher frequencies and tap into and work within higher dimensions. In this metaphysical sense, a dimension is a level of consciousness that is vibrating energetically at a particular rate/frequency; a dimension can also be considered to be a particular way of perceiving reality (explained more fully in Chapter 4).

Ascension happens naturally, but one can choose to become more fully conscious of the experience as it is happening and even accelerate the process for themselves, others and the entire planet. Since ascension involves the raising of vibration, it is about shifting from that which is of a lower or denser frequency (such as negative thinking, limited perception, personal judgements, fear and painful or suppressed emotions) to that which is of a higher or lighter frequency (such as feelings of love, joy, peace, gratitude and compassion, understanding the inter-connectedness of all things and an expanded perception of reality as a whole).

Earth is considered to be of a lower/denser vibration (3D, explained in Chapter 4) because the collective mind-set has been stuck within these lower/denser vibrating frequencies of fear and separation; but this is definitely changing.

Earth, its inhabitants and consciousness itself, is already making the transition to a higher frequency or dimension beyond the limitation of 3D. There is more to reality than meets the limited physical eye. As we raise our vibration and consciously expand our perceptions of reality, that which has been previously veiled in darkness will become illuminated by our inner awareness.

As I have already mentioned, everything is made up of energy at a fundamental level and all things are inter-connected. Underneath the surface of all that appears solid in our three-dimensional world, energy is constantly in motion; nothing is at rest. Energy differs only in degree depending on its frequency of vibration (denser/heavier - finer/lighter).

At the core of your being you are energy. Consciousness is energy. In a spiritual sense, you are not a human being having a spiritual experience; you are a spiritual being having a human experience.

The ascension experience is about the expansion of human consciousness and the shifting of vibration. When enough individual people expand their consciousness and shift into a higher frequency of vibration, a new perception of reality is co-created and a new paradigm or worldview is experienced on a collective level.

It is a far more wonderful world, a 'new world' based on moving, quite simply, from competition to co-operation and collaboration, from control to compassion and love, from greed to sharing and caring.

4

DIMENSIONS OF CONSCIOUSNESS EXPLAINED

Just like we have different dimensions in the Universe, we also have different dimensional states of consciousness as I have touched on in the previous chapter. These dimensions available to us on Earth are referred to as 3D, 4D and 5D.

These dimensions are not actual places but rather they are states of consciousness. Here on Earth, we are all living life in either 3D, 4D, 5D or a combination of all three.

In fact, it is most likely that the majority of people on Earth are moving back and forth across two or three of these dimensional states of consciousness depending on where they are in their lives.

Even though we are all living on the same planet and are surrounded by the same world, our perception of it will be different depending on which state of consciousness we are choosing to see things at.

Those perceiving things from a 3D state are going to walk through life much differently to someone perceiving things from a 5D state.

If you are curious what dimensional state your consciousness is at, here is a brief explanation of each:

Living from a 3D State

3D consciousness is viewing things from a purely physical state. You are seen as an individual that is separate from others.

Life feels like "the survival of the fittest" and you are identified by the way you look, the job you have, the car you drive and the people you surround yourself with. You may feel fearful about missing out or not having enough.

Things are perceived as being good or bad and life is a competition. There is not enough for everyone and some people have to miss out. Fulfilment is found in making money and social status.

You believe your thoughts have no power over your reality and what comes your way in life is simply a coincidence. You rely on your five senses to move through the world.

There is a lot of joy in living life from the 3D state but pain and deeper emotions can be difficult to manage.

In a 3D state there is no desire to go within or to look at things from a deeper stand point. Life is played out by skimming the surface. There is no desire to dig deep or to understand the deeper meaning behind things.

Living from a 4D State

Many people believe that the 4th dimensional state acts like a "gateway" to the 5th. When in 4D it is easy to travel back to a 3D state, however this jump in consciousness is much more difficult when you reach a 5D state.

4D consciousness begins to awaken to the idea that we are all connected and that there is more to life than meets the eye.

Thoughts are powerful and can shift the way reality is perceived. Duality and the idea of good and bad is still experienced, but there is more compassion and understanding behind it.

There is an opening to the importance of diet, meditation and leading a healthy lifestyle. What you put into your body becomes important and there is a desire to pay attention to how your actions affect the environment and those around you.

There is a strong desire to find your purpose and to follow your passions. You understand that life is meant to be enjoyed and that you are worthy to live the life of your dreams.

You perceive the world through 6 senses and your intuition starts to grow and expand. You seek a deeper meaning to life and you can start to see the synchronicity and magic of the Universe.

Living from a 5D State

Once you reach a 5D state of consciousness, it is very difficult to go back to a 3D state.

From this level of consciousness you begin to understand that we are all one and we are all connected. Life becomes an adventure of growth and there is no such thing as good or bad. There is a higher purpose for all things and every experience holds meaning.

There are stronger feelings of love and connectedness with others, the planet and even the galaxies around us. Love and compassion reign supreme and there is a lack of judgement. You understand that everyone is just on their own journey.

Everyone is considered to be equal and there is a desire to live from a place of pure authenticity. You understand that your purpose is to live your truth and to seek the joy.

From this state, you know that there is no competition and there is enough in the Universe for everyone. You feel overwhelming emotions of love and compassion for life, Mother Earth and the stars.

Your intuition is extremely strong and you feel connected to angelic and other dimensional beings/ energies.

It is important to remember that these states of consciousness are not "better" or "worse" than the other.

Every soul on this Earth has their own journey to walk and their own reasons for choosing which dimensional state to live from.

I love this explanation from an angelic source called Alariel, channelled by my friends Stuart and Joanna when they asked for a comparison between third dimensional consciousness and fifth dimensional consciousness.

"5D consciousness is essentially lighter, clearer and able to see more options and think more creatively than the 3D consciousness. It is subtler, more attuned to the holistic totality of life and less involved with individual ambitions. It thinks of the highest good of all concerned, and not about personal advantage or the opportunity to acquire or gain.

The 3D consciousness of humanity is dominated by the hopes and fears and concerns of the personality in general and the ego in particular. The ego sees no life worth having beyond its own present state of awareness, and would like to lock you into this forever, but your essential nature works against this. You have transformation written into the very fabric of your being, and you are now entering a period of rapid change. Whether the ego likes it or not, change is inevitable and is happening all around you.

The result of this change will, over time totally alter your perspective and move you from a very limited view of life, a view imprisoned by the past, to one that is open to all possibilities. The most striking practical change will be the move from a competitive economy to a co-operative social structure, from greed and accumulation to compassion and sharing.

And it is exactly this sense of sharing and community that is now arising to save your planet from its over-competitive, consumerist nightmare. The materialist paradigm is now becoming recognised for what it is — both deeply flawed and divisive socially and highly dangerous for the whole global environment.

Your science has also been evolving and your scientists are now discovering that consciousness and energy are not two separate things, but different aspects, different frequencies if you like, of one single thing. And the more powerful and developed a consciousness is, the stronger the energetic field of that person.

Here, it is a question of degree. The consciousness of the average human being is untrained, undisciplined and unfocused. It is like a diffused and weak form of light. The consciousness of a Master-soul is exactly the opposite; trained, disciplined and capable of a very exact and specific focus, like a laser beam. You can do very little with a broad and diffused beam of light, but you can do much more with a laser beam".

As I said above these states of consciousness are not "better" or "worse" than the other. Every soul on this Earth has their own journey to walk and their own reasons for choosing which dimensional state to live from. However, with the way the transformational energies and vibrations are accelerating and rising, the lower denser vibrations are going to prove challenging to exist in.

5.

STEPPING INTO 5D

By nature, we are 5th dimensional humans. This has been encoded in our DNA.

5D humans live from their heart's wisdom. They feel fully empowered and emit unconditional love and non-judgement for themselves and all others. From 5D consciousness, we know we are interconnected with all of creation as I have already mentioned.

However, over many thousands of years, most people on the planet have lost their ability to connect with this. We have ended up operating on much less than full power; we have shut down many strands of our DNA and thrust ourselves into separation consciousness, creating the situations that we currently see on earth.

Now is the time to reverse this. Now is the time to embrace the Ascension process, step into our 5D frequency and embody our 5th dimensional nature!

So how do we do this at a practical and grounded level?

I call this personal empowerment, the awakened way; the art of living, loving and thriving in this new paradigm of the fifth dimension.

It is heart based intuitive living, not mental "in the head" living. The important difference here is to release the over analysing and the micro managing of situations and events; a hard one for many I know and that has been a huge shift for me.

We have been conditioned and programmed in the old paradigm, shall we say the old operating system, that we have to "work it out" for ourselves, to take massive action consistently, it's a numbers game, you've got to work hard if you want to get anywhere and so on.

"The intuitive mind is a sacred gift and the rational mind is a faithful servant. We have created a society that honours the servant and has forgotten the gift".

Once you know how to think you will never externalise your power ever again.

It is about "BEing" rather than "DOing"; tapping into the intuitive mind and working smart not hard.

Self love and self acceptance is also a big shift for many. Learn to love and accept yourself exactly as you are and if there are parts of you, behaviours etc that you do not like, do something about it.

Treat people as you wish to be treated at all times!

Do not start worrying that if you just accept where you are right now, you are never going to get anywhere else and nothing is going to get better, that's not true! When you just accept and do not resist where you are and are grateful in this place, and appreciate that you are alive and breathing, you start to find your way in the smaller things, all the avenues of miracles and abundance, happiness and joy, open up for you.

That was a huge breakthrough for me, learning to live in the Now. Not resisting my situation, accepting it and deliberately choosing thoughts of gratitude and love, totally appreciating that THIS is the only moment I have.

We live in an eternal moment of NOW!

Remember your point of power is in the Now!

In this moment, right here, right now, at zero point, just you, your breath, this is where your power is. Not in the past with resentment, guilt and shame and not in the future with worry, anxiety and uncertainty.

This place of personal empowerment is a place of freedom and this is actually our natural default when we allow it to be so.

It is getting into flow and accessing the ability to give and receive equally; a lot of people are not in their empowerment because they do not know what it is like to receive or they do not feel worthy to receive.

You take yourself out of personal empowerment and out of an awakened way of living when you have expectations, judgements and attachments and when you are carrying others and they are not honouring their own journey.

When you start awakening and when you remember who you truly are, a perfect beautiful soul, this too creates new neural pathways and will allow you to live in a default of thriving rather than a default of stress and anxiety; in the beginning, without any of the circumstances changing in your life whatsoever!

Nothing is outside of you, you are in charge of what your vibration and frequency expresses as you step into the awakened empowered way.

How would it *feel* if you really did have everything you wanted? What would a sense of fulfilment and a feeling of being safe, loved and valued feel like?

Experience the joy in imagining this. Feel into the sensation of being able to be the very best version of yourself – where you are the most empowered, happy, and fulfilled you could ever be, doing what you most love.

Imagine what it would be like to be totally loving your life and your relationships. What would life be like if you were experiencing a constant and complete connection to Source and to all of life? How would you feel? Embrace this feeling now and hold it for as long as possible.

Instead of having to chase life, life will come to you, because your default is now to thrive.

If you are ready to step into your personal empowerment please read out loud, confidently and with positive emotion, this powerful Empowerment Prayer and visualise where guided to embed this energy.

NB I've already shared this in my book "The Power Within You Now!" however it is so powerful I feel it would be remiss of me not to include it in this book.

Empowerment Prayer
channelled from Archangel Gabriel

I am myself

I accept myself

I value myself

I forgive myself

I bless myself

I express myself

I trust myself

I love myself

I empower myself

For all the times that I have given my power away to others or to fear,

I call that power back to me NOW

From this life or any other life, from this planet or any other planet, in this dimension or any other dimension … hidden or seen … I command my power back to me NOW.

Through every photon, atom, neutron and electron … through every piece of my soul fragment; through my higher soul portal, I call back all my divine, empowerment NOW.

So just visualise now.....

Visualise waves of golden and white energy coming to you …

breathe it in …

allow the golden light of your empowerment to penetrate your skin … cocoon you in light and open your solar plexus.

Feel your power returning to you …

breathe it in …

Feel your personal empowerment ignite with every breath you take …

Feel your multi-dimensional DNA activate …

and feel the acupuncture points on your body fill with photon packages of light, assisting your DNA to remember your unique spiritual powers and innate abilities

Bask in your divine empowerment light.

Radiate your light back to the Universe and throughout the planet.

Proclaim from this moment forward … say out loud or to yourself....

Nothing can dim the light that I shine from within.

I have ignited my personal empowerment…

and now just breathe it in…

Feel your solar plexus open… you have called back all the power that you have ever given away…

and declare out loud...

And so it is…

thank you, thank you, thank you

It is done, it is done, it is done

(The End)

You may find it easier to record it onto your phone in a soothing voice, allowing time for you to repeat the statements where necessary and so that you can guide yourself through the visualised sections.

This activation is an experience, so allow yourself to feel and truly experience it. The more you can experience the activations, the more of your latent and dormant DNA that is encoded within your empowerment activates. You don't have to do anything other than just BE a fifth dimensional being!

Claim it!

The awakened way means you have got to have plenty of compassion for yourself, be kind to yourself and pick yourself up if you fall down. If anxiety comes up, allow it to be released, allow it to move through, do not wrestle with it or over analyse it, release it to source, to the angels, to God, to the light, let it go!

Be a witness, an observer, don't take anything personally! Don't take your inner critic personally, release your judgement on other people and then you won't need to take their behaviour personally, that is purely a construction of the ego.

Speak your truth, communicate and work it out in a loving and compassionate manner.

A profound knowing will emerge once you awaken to who you truly are; that you are not broken and all that programming of being told "blah blah blah" as a child or perhaps more recently, means nothing now; nothing will tether you in the third dimension!

You do not need fixing!

Remind yourself you are on the road to remembering who you truly are, an unlimited divine soul, a spiritual being having a human experience, a child of god, a goddess, whatever resonates with you.

When you can look at yourself as the Universe, God and your angels look at you, they do not see any character flaws. They see a divine beautiful soul.

People unfortunately put you into their reality, put you into a box, tether you, put you down, but that is what awakening is all about, releasing those tethers and chains so you can fly!

When you are in your personal empowerment, when you are living the awakened way you are FREE. It feels really good!

Any part of your life that you are trying to *make* happen in your life, that is very much third dimensional living; my value depends on it, my ego wants it so I am going to get it no matter what.

Meditate on how it feels in the heart to connect with the right people for you now and then take the *inspired* action, approach it spiritually, energetically, *knowing* that it is done and that everything happens FOR you not against you.

The inspired action then actually happens with ease and grace instead of running round like a headless chicken or a busy fool, doing a lot of things but not getting much done. There are too many people getting burnt out with stress in our society, their immune system shuts down and they lose clarity and focus and they literally cannot see the wood for the trees. (Been there, done that!)

Do not worry about mistakes, those 'm' words are just course adjustments, they are purposeful and driving us somewhere, do not judge them as something bad.

Take away good and bad and reframe things in your life and call them "colourful". Remember to come from a place that everything happens FOR you, it's just redirection and refocus. Trust that the universe knows what the highest vibrational trajectory is for you but you have got to be in the space to allow that to happen. Do not wallow!

Personal empowerment and stepping into your power, for some, can be a conscious fear and for many a subconscious one. Meditating, walking in nature and experiencing joy can shift that subconscious programming. Keep asking your higher self, the angels, God, (whatever is right for you) to show you and if you keep taking an honest assessment of patterns that keep re-occurring in your life, you will start to see where those subconscious programmings lie, for example "I'm not good enough".

Please remember you are just right as you are!

As I said earlier, be kind and compassionate to yourself. Don't over analyse, honour how you feel and allow it to shift through, relax and go with the flow. BE rather than DO.

The fifth dimensional portal is a space of pure potentiality, of infinite possibilities, limitlessness and miraculous healing.

The fifth dimensional portal has 2 passwords; *allow* and *surrender.*

The exciting thing is when you step into your personal empowerment you truly can create seemingly impossible miracles by allowing and surrendering.

Ask your higher self, your guides and angels to show you and, if you haven't already, develop the conscious connection between you and them.

Ask! Show me my plan or better!

Better always shows up. Be open and in a state of allowance and trust.

Trust is so important. Many know the expression "Let go and let God". It's almost like you are floating on water, you just have to have that trust. It can be so hard for us as humans to trust in something that we cannot physically see, but we all breathe air, we can't see it but we are breathing it.

Seriously, this shift for me has been huge; I used to over plan and have a need at some level to always be busy and in control.

For many, many years now my main focus has been to embrace, love and thrive in the Now, as after all, it IS the only moment we have.

Every day I walk out in nature, tune in and say to Source and the higher realms "Show me if there is anything you wish me to do and I'll do it, nudge me, make it clear to me" or words to that effect.

I relax and trust it will be shown to me in due course. In fact, the reason I was inspired to write this book is from a strong, persistent intuitive nudge, hence why I have followed through with the action.

How do you know when you are on the right path? Your heart lights up and you feel joyful.

It is this process of fully experiencing joy and the sense of having all you could ever desire that will begin to create a life filled with all that is required to bring this about.

You do not need to decide "how" this is all going to happen – just *feel the feeling* of it all already being present. If you can feel this Now as much as possible, it will accelerate your journey into 5D.

Watch what happens as you simply allow Source to fill in your new reality. Stay in the moment; make plans if necessary, but stay flexible and fluid. You may be in for some wonderful surprises.

Be aware that timelines are shifting, sometimes daily. What was originally going to take place today may have already changed. Watch to see what new events or situations arise to point you in a new direction.

Trust that Source will bring you exactly what you need in just the right timing.

The bridge between the two worlds of 3D and 5D is now getting shorter and shorter. Keep focused on the brightly lit vista ahead of you and keep walking towards it, one step after another. As you do this, feel how its pull on you gets stronger and stronger.

Know and trust that you will be guided flawlessly into your new 5D reality, a new wonderful world!

6

THE POWER OF OUR HEART'S INTUITION

We ALL have extraordinary potential, super learning and deep intuition and we can tap into this by understanding the incredible union between our heart and our brain.

While our brain releases the chemistry into our bodies for rejuvenation, healing, hormonal balance and many other things, our brain receives many of the instructions that tell us what to do from the heart. We are the ones that create the instructions through our thoughts, feelings, emotions and beliefs. Our heart has the ability to think on its own, to remember and to feel on its own as scientific studies are showing.

This information demonstrates a relatively new sense of what the heart brain connection is all about, as we have been conditioned in the past to use them independently, one or the other.

Quite simply, these two organs support a single common neural network.

We have, however, to be very clear when we're "hearing" information. Is it from our heart or is it coming from our head triggering a fear from a past memory?

There is another kind of intuition that processes information very quickly. This whole idea of deep intuition is a very powerful sense. It is a *knowing*, a direct knowing, our heart's knowing of when something is true for us and when it is not.

It took sophisticated research and modern equipment on some of the most ancient and primitive practices of Tibetan monks, for scientists to begin to understand how this form of intuition works.

They discovered that it works by using a brain state that no one knew about; indeed it was certainly not explained in textbooks.

The traditional brain states are the delta waves when we are deeply asleep, the theta waves when we are drowsy, the alpha waves when we are very relaxed and the beta waves, when we are busily engaged in daily activities.

This used to be the end of the brain states, but there is another brain state that scientists are working with and it is above the beta wave. It is called gamma.

Gamma waves are much faster and more compressed and these are the brainwaves that the Tibetan monks create in their bodies intentionally on demand, to accomplish the amazing feats of healing, of awareness and intuition. They are able to regulate their body functions, their body temperatures, their immune response and their anti aging hormones, all on demand when they choose and this is where they find their power by realising this potential.

Interestingly and perhaps not surprisingly, it is by harmonising the heart and the brain that we achieve this gamma state and we can do this intentionally.

The gamma state allows us very fast processing, storage, information and retrieval.

If we just rely on our brain for an answer, the information processing is slower. It is because the brain, before it gives us an answer, goes through all of the loops of the logic, the fears, any issues from the past, issues of self doubt and self esteem etc.

The heart, however, does not judge right, wrong, good or bad. The heart can discern what is true for us and what is not.

Gamma state is also a natural antidepressant, we are much happier and calmer and it also awakens and breathes life into our sensory perceptions. There are so many benefits of being in the gamma state and achieving heart brain coherence.

What scientists know is that every moment of every day there is a conversation between the heart and the brain. The heart is speaking to the brain, and the quality of the conversation that comes from the heart and the brain tells the brain what chemistry to release into the body (I've also touched on this in Chapter 2).

For example, when we are feeling emotions that we would typically consider negative, such as anger, hate, jealousy or bitterness, the signal from the heart to the brain is chaotic and jagged, which signals chaotic chemistry in our brain.

This is the kind of chemistry that tells us that we need high amounts of adrenaline and high amounts of cortisol, the stress hormones, to respond to something quickly in life. That can be a good thing in certain circumstances but just for a short while. We certainly do not want to live our life day in and day out like this.

When we feel emotions such as compassion, caring and gratitude the signal becomes very even, rhythmic and coherent. It sends a different signal to our brain which releases a different chemistry into our bodies. This in turn awakens our brain to send powerful healing and immune responses, powerful anti-aging hormones and so much more. It turns on the gamma state, awakens our senses and our deep intuition.

We can shift these brain states very quickly and here is a technique I learnt from Gregg Braden which enables us to tap into these potentials in our life whenever we choose to do so!

There are three simple steps:

The first step is to simply shift your awareness from your mind into your heart by gently touching your heart centre, physically, in a way that is comfortable for you with your open palm. Your awareness will always go to the place where you feel the physical sensation.

The second step is to slow your breathing. Five seconds, inhale, five seconds, exhale and continue for at least 3 minutes. The only time you would ever naturally slow your breathing and breathe in that way is when you feel safe and not threatened, so you are telling your body you are in a place that is safe.

The third step and this is the key is to begin to *feel* the field that creates the gamma state. Feel the feeling that sets up the coherence between your heart and your brain.

And how do you do that?

Scientists and researchers at the HeartMath Institute (www.heartmath.org) have found that there are four key words that work almost 100% of the time for everyone; *Appreciation* for anything or anyone, *gratitude* for anything or anyone and *care* and *compassion*.

If you can feel one or a combination of those feelings in your heart, while you are breathing as if your breath is coming from your heart, touching your heart centre, you are setting up a communication between your heart and your brain.

You are triggering neurons to begin to reach out and find other neurons to strengthen this connection.

It takes about 72 hours (three days) to build these networks. So the more you do it, the stronger this connection becomes in your life!

You can simply use this technique before you go to bed at night to sleep and trigger a healing within your body. You can do it first thing in the morning and throughout the day as and when required.

Researchers have found that typically just three minutes at a time using this technique will set into motion a cascade of events within your body, biochemical events, that can last as long as six hours.

As simple as it seems, this is a powerful key to awaken your deepest intuition and the greatest potential in your life; the doorway to all the abilities considered rare and mystical in the past.

7.
HOW DOES ASTROLOGY HELP US?

These last couple of years (2020-2022) have seen more and more people following astrology to give them hope in what has been a challenging time.

I have learnt so much personally from a great friend of mine, Pam Gregory, who is a Master Astrologer and I quote her below.

"Astrology is so profound as it is such a brilliant framework for life; it is a very practical framework and a highly spiritual framework which gives you the bigger picture. You are not just looking at the now moment, you are looking at cycles.

Pluto is a planet which has a 248 year orbit and quite simply it represents power; so whatever sign it is in, it intensifies the power of the sign it is moving through.

Since 2008 for instance, it has been moving through the sign of Capricorn; that is big business, banks, governments, corporations, institutions, the top down organisations that have had power over us.

Pluto is currently grinding through the last few degrees of Capricorn and begins to move into Aquarius in March 2023. It then goes back and forth between the end of Capricorn and beginning of Aquarius until it fully moves into Aquarius in December 2024.

Historically, if we look back to when that has happened before there is usually huge inequality between the "elite" at the top and the poor, ordinary people at the bottom. This is the situation we are in right now.

When Pluto starts to really move through those last few degrees of Capricorn, which it is right now, it will dig up any corruption, anything that is not for our highest good or of highest integrity and reveal it to the world.

This will accelerate the collapse of the old order and the old systems. Many systems will collapse; political, educational, medical, financial and legal. This is necessary because Pluto, as it starts to move into Aquarius from March 2023 onwards, is going to shift the power to the people and enable a far kinder, equal world.

However, it is important to remember that astrology is only half the picture.

It is the kit of modelling clay that is not yet formed. It is the sheet of music that is not yet played; it is raw potential.

Astrology is a language of probabilities, mathematical probabilities and it parallels the quantum principles of how reality is formed.

Our reality, our future is actually fluctuating in every moment, because we are changing our frequency individually and collectively in every moment.

So our tomorrow, we can change today, by our thinking and our emotion. It is constantly fluctuating where we are jumping from one timeline to another individually every few seconds, maybe even quicker than that.

So we really have immense power as co-creators, as astrology is only half the picture, we are the other half in how we shape the modelling clay and how we play the music.

Our attention and our focus feed, energise, activate and strengthen any potential that we then make manifest.

Focus is food energetically.

Where attention goes, energy flows and manifestation occurs."

Thank you Pam!
www.pamgregory.com

It really is up to us how we play the music. Shall we play the recorder badly or shall we thrive together in a beautiful symphony orchestra?

We can do this! We have the power within every single one of us.

Let us co-create a wonderful world for all!

8.

THE GOLDEN AGE IS COMING!

What is a golden age? A wonderfully flourishing period of peace, harmony, stability and prosperity for all.

As I write this mid 2022, there are 10 years until 2032, the start of the new golden age. There are astrological configurations and things happening in the cosmos, as they did in 2012, which heralds new energy coming in to assist this wonderful transformation.

In my Introduction I welcomed the part of you and indeed the part of me that is willing *not* to know right now every detail of *how* we can create a "Wonderful World for All".

Part of our journey to the new Golden Age is the discovery of new capacities, new sources of information and solutions. Once the new golden age is in, the consciousness shall support a totally different world. In the meantime, everything that is not in alignment with the new paradigm is collapsing.

There have been five golden ages since the birth of our planet and we are preparing now for the sixth.

The whole world, all of humanity, is now closer together energetically, via the heart field, than we have been in hundreds of thousands of years. We are closer than we have been since the last Golden Age on Earth, which has been wiped (and buried) from many of our historical texts; it was literally that long ago.

But, make no mistake, life moves in cycles and we are moving and spiralling upwards, towards another Golden Age. You may not see it in full flow in your lifetime, but you have the most important role to play within this new age, because you are here during the transition. What you say, do, think and how you act now and in the coming years, will impact humanity for centuries to come. Your life and how you use it, matters that much right now.

The new golden age *is* coming. A lot of people can feel it. Everything is coming full circle. Through great pain, something beautiful is birthed. Humanity has gone through great pain in recent times with global lockdowns etc and this has expedited the shift as more and more are choosing freedom and love over control and fear.

The truth is here and the awakening is now bigger than the illusion. A new way of living and being is birthing.

How quickly and how gloriously we bounce back from the damage of our past and build a wonderful world, where it is possible to love and grow and live without fear, depends largely on ourselves. How we handle the upcoming time will make all the difference.

With many more of humanity finally letting go of fear so much becomes possible. Imagine the changes in society just from the eradication of fear. So much of what we do is based in fear; the fear that people won't love us, won't like us, may hurt us, the fear that there won't be enough resources to survive, the fear that something bad may happen. All of this fear leads to anger, distrust, hate and abuse, which in turn leads to more fear.

Imagine, for a moment, what changes when people let that fear go and begin to find joy in themselves, in each other, in the world. It changes everything about relationships, self-image, the way we lead our lives and organise our societies and communities and relate to others all over the world.

As people operate from joy and from the heart, everything in their inner world will come to reflect it. Self-talk will be kind and supportive, rather than critical. It will be normal for people to love themselves and know they are loved, and everyone will know that they have value simply by existing, and that they don't need to prove it to themselves or anyone else. When we exercise or eat, it will be because we enjoy our bodies, rather than from shame or guilt.

People will be more spiritual and find their intuitive abilities surfacing. Imagine what happens when everyone in the world begins to be intuitive. When everyone can tell what others are feeling and no abused person, hungry child or frightened animal will be ignored any longer. When the magic and miracles we have been longing for in our dreams, start becoming reality!

And if you can, imagine a world where everyone is centred in the heart, where every person you meet in the street looks at you with equality, kindness and love and genuinely cares about you and your well-being.

Imagine every person "in power" making decisions for the best interests of others and constantly looking for new ways to help people feel safe, find joy and abundance in all things and express their uniqueness.

All the decisions taken will be on a completely new level, *by the people for the people* and for the highest good of the community.

Wow, doesn't that *feel* wonderful!

I write in this manner as just our focus on the new golden age is so powerful, it helps us all collectively to co-create the energy that we have been given. This is the possibility that is happening for us and we can co-create it by focusing on it and by absolutely knowing that it *is* coming.

A quick reminder, though, to *not* let your analytical self take over and attempt to micro-manage how this could possibly come about!

As I explained in Chapter 1, your point of power is in the NOW and the way you *feel* in *every* moment is what you are creating and the energy you are emanating and simultaneously drawing to you.

Live and thrive in the NOW...when we do this life comes to us rather than us having to chase life.

Trust the future is golden; a wonderful golden world of love and wisdom.

To conclude this chapter I am delighted and honoured that world renowned author and spiritual teacher Diana Cooper, a great friend of mine, has written this visualisation especially for my readers.

Visualisation to bring forward the new Golden Age

By Diana Cooper

Sit quietly and open your heart, radiating love around you.

You find yourself walking along a path towards a gateway to the golden future.

Open it and find yourself in a beautiful park.

People everywhere are exuding honesty, love and peace.

Feeling relaxed, comfortable and welcoming, you greet everyone with smiles and open hearts.

Enjoy feeling totally accepted and belonging.

You are going to a community meeting and join others in a large room.

You surround yourself in golden light and mentally affirm that every decision you take is for the benefit of all.

Everyone links heart to heart, with pure intention, and decisions are taken quickly and easily to the satisfaction of all.

You have plenty of leisure and make choices to do only what gives you joy and soul satisfaction.

You relax knowing that in the 5th dimension all that you need comes to you automatically.

Visualise how you spend your time.

Then notice how you enjoy caring and sharing.

How do you look after nature and animals?

What does it feel like to live, work and relax with people on your wavelength?

Now bring back this energy into your life.

And seek out others on your wavelength, with whom you feel respected and a belonging.

Take decisions from the heart for the highest good of everyone.

Bring more fun and creativity into your life.

Spend time caring and sharing.

And look after nature and animals.

Then open your eyes and live at a higher frequency.

Diana also suggested I include her Vision Prayer that she wrote for her book "2012 and Beyond".

The Vision Prayer

I have a vision where all people are at peace, fed and housed.

Every child is loved and educated to develop their talents.

Where the heart is more important than the head

And wisdom is revered over riches.

In this world justice, equality and fairness rule.

Nature is honoured,

So the waters flow pure and clear and the air is fresh and clean.

Plants and trees are nurtured

And all animals are respected and treated with kindness.

Happiness and laughter prevail

And humans walk hand in hand with angels.

Thank you for the love, understanding, wisdom, courage and humility

To do my part to spread the light.

May all the world ascend.

So be it.

Thank you Diana!

www.dianacooper.com

9.

IT'S ALREADY BEGINNING!

A new wonderful world is already emerging, but whether you see this or not is largely down to where you put your focus.

For anyone watching the mainstream news, I think you will agree with me there is never, or rarely, anything positive reported. It is rather fear driven to say the least. I stopped watching a long time ago for this reason.

Indeed, I am observing some major shifts occurring in how so many people are viewing their lives, the old systems and services and are making headway towards positive change.

One of these areas is on the subject of health and I asked my friend, Dr. Sam White, to contribute to this book....

"As I write this I am currently en route overseas to lecture on the "Future of Healthcare". The timing could not be more appropriate for my contribution to my friend Sue's book.

Put simply the current medical model is unsustainable. The way in which allopathic doctors look at dis-ease is both a combination of overly simplistic and needless complicated (polypharmacy- i.e. patients on seemingly endless prescription medicines).

We are all unique, sentient beings with an incredible and unlimited ability to create and thus a seemingly infinite number of medical variances based upon factors including (but not limited to) our genetics and epigenetic expression.

The latter is of course determined by a combination of our environment which comprises our physical, emotional and psychological experience. Thus, to have our health and wellbeing filtered down to a 10-minute consultation and mere tick box exercise rarely provides satisfaction for either the doctor or patient.

A pill to treat the symptoms of a condition is not necessarily addressing the actual cause of the problem. Many have come to accept taking a pill as the norm; but not anymore.

We stand at the precipice of what I refer to as "the Great Awakening"; a mass realisation that something is not quite right and perhaps never has been. This realisation extends equally to the basis of a medical system over-reliant on ever more expensive and toxic drugs. In the West today iatrogenic death (i.e. caused by a medical intervention) ranks third as the leading cause of death. This must stop.

My own awakening regarding the current medical system began a few years ago whilst working as a busy primary care physician (GP). At the relatively young age of just 32 I too became unwell. Daily life became an enduring struggle. It wasn't long before I realised that even my own knowledge and experience was entirely insufficient to help me to help myself. At the same time, I realised an ever-greater number of my own patients would "slip through the net" of modern day flawed medical modelling. Their unique combination of symptoms simply did not tick a box and thus both they and I could not get the answers we so desperately needed.

If I was to truly help others and even get myself back on track, I needed to find an alternative. That's when I first began learning and studying Functional Medicine. Such medicine combines ancient wisdom with modern day scientific reasoning and is root cause focused. Symptoms are merely clues; as Functional Doctors we look at the real reason symptoms develop.

A typical patient to my clinic is someone "who has been around the houses" or "pushed from pillar to post". They have often seen innumerable specialists and had endless tests. Some have been harmed by their allopathic management. Of the patients I see almost none have derived any sustained benefit thus far and are in despair and feel without hope.

Likewise, I too spent time seeing different specialists-all without any answers. Why? It all comes down to the quality of the questions asked. That is where functional medicine is different. To give an example, do you really think depression is caused by a Prozac deficiency? Likewise, high cholesterol is not a statin deficiency. Both indicate something else is going on. Why not go in search of *that* something?

Following preliminary investigations we build a plan toward healing and their very good long-term health- all without pharmaceuticals.

With the right support and a functional based approach, they can be shown how to live a life free of pain and suffering and without medication.

Functional Medicine is by no means an overnight fix and requires a lot of commitment on the part of the patient. But for me personally, this is what medicine was always intended to be and what we must seek to return to. It is truly patient focused and will be our healthcare for the future."

Thank you Sam!

Dr Sam White   www.drsamwhite.com
Functional Medical Doctor MBChB
Member of ILADS and IFM Board Member for Children's Health Defence U.K

Dr. Sam is also an Ambassador for the People's Health Alliance (www.the-pha.org), which is an incredible example of a people led project founded by visionary Katherine Macbean and others in April 2022.

This grassroots organisation has created an integrative healthcare model to heal, support and empower the people. They encourage local communities to set up their own local hubs filled with knowledgeable practitioners who offer a range of individualised health services.

Within just a matter of months over 125 hubs have been established in the UK and the model has spread to over 25 countries across the world.

They utilise allopathic and holistic treatments, harnessing nature and re-discovering traditional medicine.

They support physical wellbeing as well as emotional and spiritual wellbeing; a wonderful recipe for optimal vibrant living!

For eons all over the world there have been incredible groups of people doing wonderful things for humanity, the animals and the planet, and more and more new grassroots up initiatives are forming right now.

Many are coming together in their local groups, collaborating and building supporting community hubs and assemblies set up and run *by the people for the people.* The devastating, for many, loss of trust in governments around the world has expedited this.

These currently exist all over the UK and in other countries. Each community hub incorporates many projects including growing, enterprise, lawful, learning and indeed health.

The genuine care, kindness, collaboration and support I've witnessed within these communities is truly heart-warming.

There are many community grow projects around the country. One of these I've witnessed firsthand as my twin sons Rich and Nick established Nourish Community (www.nourishcommunity.co.uk) in 2020.

It is a not-for-profit large organic vegetable garden which they set up to enable people, from all walks of life, access to healthy and organic food.

They collaborate with other local community projects, helping, in particular, people on low or no income.

They also give talks within the communities and schools; inspiring and educating others to get more involved with food growing projects, and to understand the key skills in becoming more self and community sustainable.

In addition, The People's Food and Farming Alliance (www.the-pffa.org), also founded by Katherine Macbean, aims to connect communities with local farmers and growers through educational support, common sense accreditation, local and regional distribution and by ensuring a natural approach to food production.

These are just a few real life examples that I know of personally demonstrating the way of the new heart-led world; everywhere I look more and more are passionate about doing something to truly make a difference, not only in their own lives but in the lives of others.

Knowing what we know about energy, vibration, intention coupled with action, exponential growth in so many areas will be unstoppable!

The 100th Monkey Effect comes to mind!

If you haven't come across it before, the hundredth monkey phenomenon is a sociological theory. It dates back to a study in 1952 which followed the behaviour of a hungry young female monkey living in the wild on a Japanese island.

One day, no doubt fed up with the residual taste of grit in her mouth after mealtimes, she had a bright idea; she washed her dirt-encrusted potatoes in the sea before eating them. Her family watched on, curiously, then followed suit, then her playmates and then their families. One-by-one this culture change spread.

But it was what scientists reportedly observed next that was remarkable. This new idea went from being an exception when the 100th monkey copied the behaviour. Within no time at all every monkey on the island took it as the norm and monkeys on other islands automatically did the same!

It is what is now described as the point at which "critical mass" had been reached … the tipping point for all other monkeys to follow suit.

Quite simply, this 100th Monkey phenomenon means that when a limited number of individuals knows a new way and as more individuals manifest this new awareness, the energetic field of consciousness is strengthened and a critical mass is reached.

Watch this space! Our loving, caring, sharing world is emerging.

10.
POWERFUL SELF TALK

I thought I would conclude this short practical book by sharing my favourite affirmations, which have proved to be beyond powerful for me.

I create seemingly impossible miracles.

By saying "seemingly impossible" it bypasses your conscious and subconscious minds that may try and tell you it is not possible!

Thank you for giving me all the wisdom, knowledge and guidance I need to do what I am here to do.

I love life and life loves me!
Thank you, thank you, thank you.

I am rich beyond my wildest dreams,
I am, I am, I am.
I am rich beyond my wildest dreams
in love and joy and health and wealth,
thank you, thank you, thank you!

I have been saying these for years and they are very true for me, but if you are not quite feeling it yet I suggest saying it many times a day to begin with.

If you say it enough and cultivate the e-motion (energy in motion) aligned with it, before you know it you will be living it NOW.

It also shifts your focus to be "solution" conscious rather than "problem" conscious.

A thought and statement repeated over and over again eventually gets accepted as a belief....the more you do it the quicker you start seeing results.

Last thing at night I go outside, look at the sky and say out loud.....

Thank you beautiful, magical sky I always keep my vibration high!

If it's a clear starry night it feels even more powerful!

In addition, in my book "The Power Within You Now!" I share in detail why I believe having your own unique "Life Mission Statement" is a short cut to creating miracles and a life you love.

The "shortcut" is to nourish your mind with *powerful positive feeling* words and emotions.

Remember, this is ancient wisdom backed up by science. The heart is the strongest biological generator of electrical and magnetic waves and is 5,000 times more powerful than the brain magnetically!

Here is an example of a Life Mission Statement relevant for these times, which of course you can personally tweak accordingly.

By saying "Every day in every way and in every moment" it gently drip feeds your subconscious mind to accept this new instruction and create this as your reality.

Every day in every way and in every moment I am so grateful for all the amazing good in my life right now.
I love and accept myself.
I am whole and I am complete.
I am totally happy and I am at peace.
I am confident, empowered and fulfilled and I am abundant and successful in all areas of my life.
I am thriving and I am free.
I am strong and I am courageous.
I am love and I am compassion.
I am caring and I am sharing.
I am vibrant and I am energised.
I am healthy; mentally, emotionally, physically and spiritually.
My world and the world at large are thriving as one more than I ever imagined possible.
I love life and life loves me!
Thank you, thank you, thank you!

Please trust me; this "stuff" is powerful!

Changing beliefs and cultivating belief in yourself takes "work" but my goodness is it worth the effort! As soon as you start to truly believe in yourself, life can take off....and please remember that everyone has the capability to learn how to change their beliefs.

Dare to dream, set the intention and cultivate the belief too that we can ALL live a wonderful life.

Open yourself up and tap into the pure limitless potentiality by feeling the e-motion of gratitude, peace, joy and love....with practice this IS possible.

As you raise your individual vibration, your strong and powerful consciousness helps raise the collective consciousness as well.

It is true that we *can* change the world by changing ourselves.

Let's BE the change we wish to see in the world.

A Wonderful World for All is emerging!

Thank you, thank you, thank you.

ACKNOWLEDGEMENTS

Thank you beautiful Honfleur, my place of writing, for your love and inspiration as always.

Thank you to Corrine Cyster for finding the perfect heart shaped diamond for my book jacket and thank you to Victoria Jones for the full design of the cover.

Thank you to Aimee Joy Photography for my profile picture.

NOTES

NOTES

NOTES